FINISHING LINE PRESS

www.finishinglinepress.com

THE DISTANCE IS MORE THAN AN OCEAN
—a travelogue memoir

by

Chris Wiewiora

Finishing Line Press
Georgetown, Kentucky

THE DISTANCE IS MORE THAN AN OCEAN
—a travelogue memoir

ACKNOWLEDGMENTS

My thanks to the editors of the following publications where pieces of *The
Distance Is More Than An Ocean* first appeared:

A River & Sound Review
Airplane Reading
Redivider
Slice
Two Countries: U.S. Daughters & Sons of Immigrant Parents

Publisher: Leah Maines
Editor: Christen Kincaid
Cover Art: Dan Folgar
Author Photo: Kristin Houser
Cover Design: Elizabeth Maines McCleavy, Dan Folgar

Printed in the USA on acid-free paper.
Order online: www.finishinglinepress.com
              also available on amazon.com

Author inquiries and mail orders:
Finishing Line Press
P. O. Box 1626
Georgetown, Kentucky 40324
U. S. A.

For my grandmothers:
Lois Flanagan Almond & Anna Wilczynska Wiewiora Dumas
(1922 - 1996 & 1929 - 2016)

For a beginning
let yourself be drawn like debris
to all the great bodies of water;
I will be there
asking you to help
lift up a hand of water
and reach into a time
we dream to change.
No matter that even before
your first palm is taken away
the water washes off itself
like quicksilver off a wall of glass
or that your hand becomes a broken colander
wired loosely to the wrist,
sieving whatever drifts by,
no matter—we also want to keep an eye peeled
for anything that might give the past away:
bits and pieces, twigs and such.
We can begin anywhere
you find an entry.

Excerpt of "Patching Up the Past with Water" from Water
Tables © *1974 by James Seay. Published by Wesleyan
University Press and reprinted with permission.*

At my parents' dining room table, I spin the Lazy Susan, and a matryoshka orbits the saltshaker in the middle. The hollow wooden nesting doll with its lacquered, babushka-covered head blurs and then slows, and stops. I pick up the doll and pull her torso off from her stumpy legs. Another, smaller babushka doll sits inside of the first one. I open her up until I'm left with a solid thumb-sized doll.

I'm waiting while Dad proofs an essay of mine about growing up overseas. Mom washes dishes by hand at our stainless steel sink. Even though we moved to Florida almost twelve years ago, she says she can't get used to having a dishwashing machine. Mom always does the laundry as well as the dishes before bed. In Poland, the Communists used to scale down the electricity and cut the water off at night.

Mom pulls her left hand out of the water to push her glasses up the bridge of her nose. A purple scar cuts along her finger from an injury in a car wreck last summer. She likes to soak her hand in the sudsy warm water.

Mom is paying for Dad and me to fly to Poland with money from the wreck's insurance settlement. She says it'll be a good father and son trip for us to do. It'll be my first time back since third grade.

I consider my last day in Poland as my ninth birthday. Outside, I played blind man's bluff with my friends. They hid behind the trellis, but couldn't go as far as the apricot tree. The sweet pulp from dropped, over-ripe fruit filled the backyard.

Inside, white boxes filled our living room. In big black letters, the names of cities were printed on all the sides of the boxes. Only two cities mattered to me: WARSAW and ORLANDO.

The wax from nine lit candles melted as my friends sang "*Sto lat*/Good Luck," with lyrics that mean, "Live for a hundred years." I blew out the candles. The smoke curled into the air.

At the dining table, Dad hands me back my essay. The word *because* is circled in a sentence that reads *We moved back to the States, because my grandmother died.* In the margin, he made a question mark, and also wrote *around the time.*

"What's wrong with *because*?" I ask.

"You wrote it as if it's why we came back," Dad says.

"But that's the reason," I say.

"We were already planning to come back," Mom says from the kitchen. She unplugs the drain in the sink and then flips on the garbage disposal, which gnashes the scraps that can't be saved for leftovers.

I can't argue over the noise. Mom flips the switch off. Everything grinds to a halt.

"Grandma died and then we came back," I say. For the past twelve years, I've been saying that.

"Don't you remember?" Mom asks. She dries her hands on a dishtowel. She sits down across from Dad.

"My mother died after your birthday," Mom says. "She waited, but we were already coming back."

I consider the boxes. Were the cities and the route already planned? Mom and my brother Joe were already in America. Dad and I stayed to pack.

Now, Dad and I are going back, but I don't want dates and facts. I want to keep the memory in my mind: I stood older in our Warsaw kitchen. The cold tile under my bare feet sucked out my skin's warmth from celebrating. Everything was so bright and happy. Then, Dad told me Grandma had died and I stared out the window at the light filtering through the translucent glass.

§§

I sat on gray carpet. Cutout letters of the alphabet were strung above the blackboard. Other kids repeated the teacher, "Ah."

I knew the sound wasn't connected to the letter. The teacher made a noise like the one Mom made getting into the bathtub at home. The only reasons Mom said we could disturb her soak was if we were bleeding or dying.

"Eh," I made the correct sound like the Canadians at the international church when they wanted clarification or for someone to agree with them.

The teacher ignored me.

"Bi," she said.

The other kids repeated her.

I said, "Be" and elongated it to buzz around the room like *Maya the Bee*. Each night, Joe and I watched a half-hour of *Dobranoc/ Goodnight*. When the VCR's clock blinked 20:00, we sat in front of the blank TV screen, one of us pressed the "on" button, and then we sang to the theme songs of the cartoons that were kept in English before the Polish narrator dubbed over the shows' voices.

The teacher looked at me.

"Sa," she said.

If I knew anything, then I knew how to say the first letter of my name.

"Cee," I said. It sounded the same as "see." I wanted to shout SEE! Couldn't she see I was an American? It didn't matter if Mom and Dad had brought our family to Poland, because they were missionaries. I was born in America. And even if Dad was Polish, Mom wasn't, and I wasn't going to speak Polish.

"Da," the teacher said, looking at me.

I stared at the gray carpet. I plucked the pilled up bunches of woven material. I tore the pieces out until the teacher was done saying the wrong sounds.

I knew it was lunchtime when I saw some of the other kids take out plastic bags and line up at the door. I had brought my Teenage Mutant Ninja Turtles lunchbox. I followed the other kids led by our teacher down the hallway.

I felt smaller than I usually did as a kid, because it didn't matter if I was a loudmouth. I couldn't be understood. I kept quiet and followed.

I walked at the back of the line. We went down a staircase into a basement. The windows let in a pale light. Kids without bags grabbed bowls and then had something that looked like cabbage and broth plopped into them. At the line's end, a table held a stack of pastries made of spirals of browned dough with flakes of glaze and a dollop of custard or a scoop of fruit.

I didn't have any złoties. I only had the lunch Mom packed for me. I went back to the classroom with nothing. I walked over to a corner and sat with my back to the wall. I opened up the clasps of my lunchbox.

On top Mom had set a note: *As long as I'm living my baby you'll be.* I could already read, and the sentence was from a book she read to me before bed as I cuddled in her lap. The story followed a mother who would cradle her son each night and sing the words from the note.

I shoved the note in my pocket and wiped my nose with

the cuff of my sleeve. Mom had made me a peanut butter and jelly sandwich. Wedged between the PB&J and my thermos of juice was a box of California raisins.

I couldn't understand most of what the kids were saying as they ate and played. They weren't all Poles. Many of them were Indian kids chattering away, and there were a few Asian kids that Mom had told me were Thai.

A Thai girl walked over to me. She waved her hand. I opened up the box of raisins and chewed one. I opened my hand and dumped some of the raisins out and then offered them to her, saying, "Raisin." She smiled and took them, one by one. When she ate them all, she said, "Raisin." I shook the rest of the raisins into my hand and offered her them. She took them and then finished again. "Raisin," she said. I shook my head and showed her the empty box. She walked away.

§§

At the Warsaw Chopin Airport's gate, a man stands with his chest out. The wide expanse of his middle, covered in an unzipped leather jacket, stretches at the wool of his seaweed green sweater. The man smiles at Dad in recognition.

"*Cześć, Zdzichu,*" Dad says. The Polish sounds like "Chest, G-who."

Dad and Zdzichu hug. I've only seen Dad hug family that way—full and tight. Zdzichu is one of the nationals who still worked in the missionary organization that Mom and Dad had helped establish in Poland. Zdzichu was part of Christ's family and so were my parents.

"*Krzysiu,*" Zdzichu says my childhood nickname that sounded like "Shess-who."

I want to say, "I'm not the kid I was twelve years ago." Instead, I zip up my jacket and stick my hands in my pocket, avoiding both a hug and a handshake. I say, "Hi."

"It has not been so good weather," Zdzichu says.

"Really?" Dad asks.

"It has rained, but I hear it will be sunny," Zdzichu reports.

As I wait by the luggage carousel for my bag, I consider how people talk about the weather to continue conversation's sound instead of allowing for silence. I zone out as I stare at the luggage carousel.

Back when the international airport was called Warsaw Okęcie, Dad and I checked in blue leather suitcases with metal nubs that scraped along the linoleum floor. Our dog Patch and Mom's two cats Fun and Nora yowled in their crates. Since then, our pets all died and were buried in the sandy ground of our backyard in Orlando while the luggage deteriorates in the Florida heat of our attic.

Dad pulls our bags off the conveyer belt. Zdzichu takes my

bag, opens its collapsible handle, and then leads us out into the parking lot.

"We'll want to exchange money," Dad says.

"Oh yes, yes," Zdzichu says. "We will go to the—" He stops, lost on a word.

"Bank?" Dad guesses.

"No, no. It is a place with better rates." Zdzichu says, trailing off as he glances around the parking lot. "Ahh, yes," Zdzichu says, guiding us to his car. Then he says the word he was thinking of in Polish.

Dad sits up front. He and Zdzichu babble back and forth like the wipers flicking the rain off the windshield. I don't remember enough of the language to follow their conversation.

Zdzichu drives up onto a sidewalk and parks beside a row of tin kiosks guttering water off of their ruffled roofs. We walk along a snaking asphalt path. In worn out spots, murky brown water pools. Zdzichu points to the closed shutters with padlocks.

"This is Worker's Day," Zdzichu says, "But no one is working." He laughs and Dad chuckles.

Dad notices that I don't get the joke.

"It's funny because the Communists made up the holiday," Dad says.

"Yes, but now it is celebrated as Constitution Day," Zdzichu says. He opens his arms wide, and then drops them back to his sides.

We walk farther to a storefront with a closed door. The lights are turned off. Zdzichu raises his palm over his eyes to peer inside through a window. He raps his knuckles on the glass and then twists the locked doorknob.

"It is closed," Zdzichu says. "We must go somewhere else."

As we return to the car, I notice Dad places his hand over his chest like he's going to say the Pledge of Allegiance. I realize he's checking his money pouch around his neck and tucked inside his shirt. I put my hand in the front pocket of my jeans, touching my wallet and passport.

As Zdzichu drives us, I remember how I mostly used money in Warsaw on Saturday mornings when I went to our neighborhood's corner store. I redeemed the deposit on empty glass cola bottles and then bought a Sprite for me and a Coke for Joe. I clutched the cool green neck between my thumb and forefinger and the clear bottle tinted with black caramel soda between my middle and ring fingers. In my other hand I held a box. Inside the box, a small Snickers bar fit snug against a stack of pogs with pictures of soccer players printed on them.

Back at our house, I elbowed the bell at the fence until Dad buzzed the front gate. In the kitchen I ate the Snickers as Dad uncapped the bottles. I pocketed the pogs in my sweatpants and then I walked up the wooden staircase. At the landing, I pivoted around the wobbly banister knob. In our bedroom, Joe climbed down from his top bunk and I handed him the Coke.

Down the hall, we sat on the floor of the entertainment room. Joe turned on the TV and flipped to the cartoon *Biker Mice from Mars*. We brothers thought we came from another planet, too. The Polish narrator spoke for all the English voices. Still, the dubbing couldn't completely cover over our language. I cranked up the volume.

§§

The film of water on top of the school's puke-green tiles was cold. I walked on my tippy toes trying to touch less of it. I wore trunks and held a rubber cap.

The swim teacher's belly hung over his Speedos and a necklace with a crucifix lay on the manger of his hairy chest. He blew a whistle. He pantomimed for me to pull on my cap.

I put it on and followed the other boys putting on their nose plugs. We jumped into the pool. Water filled my ears but I didn't shake it out.

I held onto the edge and kicked. I wanted to swim up and out of the pool onto the tiles and through the halls and across the parking lot and then plunk into the Wisła. I would swim across the Atlantic we flew home over summer. I couldn't wait through winter and spring in that school. I needed to go to America. I would go up the Mississippi. Up was the same as north. I would go up, and then right. Right would be to West Virginia. Almost heaven, away from Poland. I would swim down the hills to my grandparents' house in Buckhannon with strawberry patches. I would choose to live with Mom's parents, not Dad's mom, Grandma in Chicago where she spoke Polish. I would swim to my Grandma and Grandpa Almond. Home.

I would ask Grandpa Almond to fix me. He had been a doctor. Maybe he could halve the Polish.

In the pool, I breathed in water. I choked, and then gulped down more. If I filled my body with water, then maybe I could become a fish and swim back to America.

I felt two hands haul me up and out of the pool. I thrashed. The water foamed. My body slapped against the tiles and a hand smacked between my shoulder blades. I threw up.

§§

After exchanging dollars for złoties, Zdzichu drives Dad and me to an apartment building with a grocer on the other side of the street. Inside the apartment building, we cram into an elevator as small as a bathroom stall with the same sort of graffiti and rank, sticky pools in the corner. When the lattice gate closes, it triggers the clanking lift. A single light bulb illuminates us. Zdzichu, Dad, and I huddle in the middle with our personal space compromised, our shadows overlap.

At the landing, Zdzichu knocks on a door and a girl opens it.

"Hello," the girl says. Her hair is pulled back into a greasy ponytail. I notice childhood merging into teenagehood. Baby fat melts into curves and pimples mix with freckles. She wears the uniform of youth: jeans and a T-shirt.

"Joasia," Zdzichu says, which sounds like, "Yo-ash-ah."

"I'm Asha," she says and then sticks out her hand to me. "Nice to meet you."

"*Cześć*," I say. As I shake her hand, I add, "Actually, we've met before."

I remember when on furlough stateside, Asha's parents came to visit my parents in Florida. Her parents wanted to go to the beach, and so they took Joe and me along with them. Asha wiggled in a car seat between my brother and me.

Asha's father drove to Cocoa Beach where the green waves mixed their sand and shale into a harsh shoreline. Because he didn't want to pay a daily fee, he parked at a public access lot without bathrooms or even a foot-washing station; only a boardwalk led from the asphalt lot to the beach. Joe and I got out of the car, already wearing our trunks with towels slung around our necks.

Asha's parents pulled down her pants. I turned away. Joe started walking toward the sand.

Asha's parents kept her at the shoreline. Thankfully, they put her into a swimsuit. Where she sat, the water rushed up to her legs. Joe and I filled a pail with wet sand for her to make a sandcastle. Then, we splashed deeper into the water to bodysurf the waves.

When it was time to leave, Asha stayed seated at the shore. Her father told her that we were leaving with or without her. Asha turned around from her father and began to slap the water.

Asha's mother walked ahead with Joe. Asha's father began to walk away. I stayed between them still on the wet sand.

Asha turned around and saw her parents' backs turned to her. She got up and ran past me onto the dry sand. She grabbed her father's hand with both of hers.

Dad goes to the bathroom and I stand while Asha sits in the kitchen where she sips tea. The electric kettle churns with refilled water even though I didn't ask for a cup. I don't have anything to say to Asha about my memory and how she is older, but looks defiantly the same. I consider talking about the weather, but then the toilet flushes and Dad reappears. He says something in Polish.

"I speak English fine," Asha says, and then adds, "If you prefer."

"Either/or," Dad says. "I'm ready for a nap."

"I'm tired, too," I say. My mind feels worn from trying to find the meaning of Polish words in sentences like shapes in clouds. I can't believe I'm back in Warsaw and everything seems so normal but also slightly changed like Asha.

She leads us into the living room and then leaves, closing the double doors behind her. On top of an old rug, a mattress with blankets and pillows takes up most of the wooden floor. Light comes through the lace curtains over the window behind a sheet-covered couch. Bookcases line the walls. I notice several C.S. Lewis translations and theological texts on the shelves.

Dad lies down on the couch. I stretch out on top of the mattress. I stare up at the low ceiling, which feels like it presses down. I close my eyes and imagine myself back at the Orlando International Airport when everything felt open. Dad and I rode the monorail from the terminal to the gate. I remained standing and held onto a pole while Dad sat at the end of the caboose in a hollowed-out space.

Through the tinted glass I watched the last days of spring fade into the beginning of summer. Egrets drifted onto the airport's retention ponds. Palm fronds waved in the same wind. Inside, the air conditioning blasted and a robotic voice blared over the intercom something about having a safe trip.

After takeoff, I looked down to spot the cluster of giant steel stick-figure sculptures at the departure drop-off and arrivals pick-up. One figure held its I-beam arm pointing up. Another figure held its hand over its brow following the trajectory of our dissipating jet stream's trail.

On the mattress, I listen to Dad breathing steady from the couch. His rhythm is momentarily interrupted as the kettle whistles. He snores again when it's clicked off.

§§

Mom and I had walked past the Marines guarding the door. Kids and their parents hugging on their way inside all spoke English. Mom and I sat in the principal's office, because Mom had called Grandma Almond. I didn't know if Mom just told Grandma about me almost drowning at the other school, but Grandma had sent money for me to enroll at the American School.

Mr. Roland, the principal, wore a white button-up shirt, a red tie, and dark pants. He reminded me of Grandpa Almond. Mr. Roland even had reddish hair. Grandpa Almond was called Doc or Red around town, even though he had retired and his hair was now white.

Mom signed forms. The secretary made a copy of my American passport with my blond mop in the photo that didn't match my hair anymore. I had begun to brown since going to the other school. I swung my feet slung over the chair imagining pumping my legs out on the swings that I had seen in the playground.

Mr. Roland tapped the stack of forms on top of his desk, evening them all out equally.

"Your Mom says you can read a little already," Mr. Roland said.

"A lot," I said. My voice sounded loud. I was beginning to be the boy I had been. Mom was always reminding me to use my inside voice again.

"Alright now," Mr. Roland said. He nodded at Mom. "There's always a question for new students to get into the American School of Warsaw. You have to spell one thing." He held up his pointer finger.

"Okay," I said.

"Spell *Mississippi*," Mr. Roland said.

I stared at him.

"It's a river," Mr. Roland said.

Of course I knew it was a river. I knew it was a state, too. I knew it was in America. But I didn't know how the spell it.

I felt dunked underwater and gulping. Grandma had already paid all the money. Mom had filled out all the forms. I wanted to speak English. I was an American. I wanted to say I was Mississippi!

But I was Polish and I felt dumb. I couldn't speak Polish and couldn't spell English. I didn't belong at either school.

"Okay, okay," Mr. Roland said. He put his open hand out and then said, "Nothing to get in a huffy about."

Mom placed her hand on my shoulder. It felt like being pulled from the pool. I held down the urge to throw up.

"Em, eye. S, s, eye. S, s, eye. Pee, pee, eye," Mr. Roland sung the spelling. "You'll never forget it. Welcome."

§§

Warsaw isn't as I remember it. The sky should be cement-gray, but it's as beautiful as an Orlando spring afternoon. A slight breeze swirls wisps of clouds in the sky-blue sky.

The tram, clacking along its tracks, shifts Dad and me back and forth in a rocking, swaying motion, and then comes to a stop. Dad and I get off the tram at this stop, next to a field of dandelions. Some still have their yellow mane of petal clumps while others sprout their hundred-puff beards. I used to pluck their stems and blow out the puffs like birthday candles, the seeds floating up and away like a smoky wish.

Dad and I walk through the field. A dirt path cuts from the tram's stop to a road. Dad taught me how to ride my bike here. He would hold the handlebars and my seat while he ran along beside me. Then he only held onto my seat, allowing me to steer. Finally, he just placed his hand on my back, and then let me go.

The road leads into our neighborhood. The houses huddle next to each other. Not crowded, but snug behind gates and fenced-in front yards. Roots push up the sidewalk blocks and split the asphalt road with creases like palm lines. An umbrella of willow boughs filter the sunlight into strands of amber yellow.

I remember the bus stops with babushka-ed ladies on the way to market, men driving diesel Mercedes and Volvos blinking their *TAXI* signs, and children in socks and leather sandals that walked by our fence to the Polish school that I had thought looked like a Styrofoam box for leftovers.

Dad and I come to the start of our street, *Miączynska*. I can't recall how to count in Polish, but I can still recite the address of our home: *dwadzieścia-pięć*/twenty-five.

The ever-peeling white birch tree still stands behind our house's gate. I remember how Joe and I used to play soccer: I would stand at the bottom of the driveway, my hands spread out in a jumping jack, unable to defend both sides of the goal, which was the garage door behind me. It seemed like an eighty-degree slant up to Joe at the top of the driveway. Joe could only manage to lob the ball down with the inside of his foot, no swift-kicked strikes. I had to bunt the ball with the toe of my sneaker at his goal, the gate. There was no danger of my shots soaring into the street, because the spikes on top of the fence were so high that they seemed to chomp at the clouds.

Dad and I approach the fence. When I stand in front of our house, the gate hardly reaches my shoulders. The spikes are just nubs. Now, if I stood in the middle of the driveway with my arms fully outstretched, then I could grip each side of the doorframe. I don't even know if a *Maluch*/toddler Polski Fiat could fit in the driveway. And the driveway has barely any slant; closer to a thirty-five degree angle, if that. I could easily launch a ball up and over the fence and into the sky.

As my memory collapses I grasp to remember something else that is true from when we lived there. In the mornings, I would wake up to the metallic buzz of Dad's electric razor. I stood outside the bathroom, waiting for Dad to come out so I could see his face, afraid he had shaved off his mustache. I would watch the steady light peek underneath the bottom of the shut door.

I can't recognize our old home as much as I couldn't recognize Dad with a thickening gray beard during our travels so far. Dad had accidentally left the American-to-European adapter for his electric razor. Before our tram ride today to the old neighborhood, Dad bought an adapter and shaved.

I felt better then about Dad, but now I question replacing more childhood memories of our old house. Still, Dad rings the buzzer. We came all this way, but there isn't an answer.

§§

During the week, I didn't speak Polish at the American School. My Polish carpool driver—who always wore a leather jacket, T-shirt, blue jeans, and sneakers—sang clipped versions of his American rock 'n' roll tapes on the way there. "I get...Satisfaction!" On Sundays our family went to the international church, where they served tea after the service, but everything was in English. For lunch, we went to the American Club at the U.S. Embassy. I showed my new American passport with my darker hair at the guarded front entrance. Joe and I watched American cartoons in the kids room while we waited for our orders of burgers, fries, and Welch's Grape Soda.

Mom and Dad said they were afraid I would lose the language, but I had never fully had it and I didn't want any of it. I could read and spell in English. Both Mom and Dad always spoke English to me. I only spoke English to Joe. Everyone else could speak Polish for me.

Still, I sat in the living room across from the Polish tutor my parents had hired.

When she had said, "*Cześć*," I said, "Hi."

Mom sat with us and nudged me each time the tutor showed me a flash card with a photo. I was supposed to say the word in Polish. Even though I didn't want to speak Polish, I still knew it. I took my time staring at the picture of the dog.

My parents had looked for a dog for Joe and me. Even though Mom had cats, my parents thought American boys should grow up with a dog. We had gone with them to attend dog shows where greyhounds raced around tracks after an elastic band that was looped around a pole and then strung and looped to another pole. The dogs ran after a flag attached to the end of the elastic that zipped forward and then unspooled to zip to the next pole. We had driven out to the country and seen packs of German shepherd mixes guarding junk piles, their pups yipping through the rusty metal. We had visited a breeder who had sheepdogs with hair that hung over their eyes, causing them to bump into furniture around the house. We hadn't wanted any of those dogs. Joe and I had thought the search for a dog was over.

Then, one day, I came home from the American School and saw this dog running back and forth behind our front fence. The dog looked like Grandpa Almond's collies that he always named Briar. We chose to name the dog Patch.

When neighborhood kids walked by and noticed our new dog, they asked, practicing their English, "What is the name?" I told them, "Patch," but they said, "*patrz*" and gave a thumbs-up. I didn't understand until Dad explained that the Polish meant, "You watch." The other kids thought it was clever naming Patch our watchdog. But we had named him for the large spot on his coat and because we wanted to think of Grandpa Almond's strawberry patches in West Virginia.

"*Krzysiu*," Mom said. I didn't respond. I stared out the window.

Joe ran around the backyard with Patch barking after him. He knew enough Polish to talk to people on the street. I watched Patch jump up. Joe said, "Down." We even taught our dog English, so why did I have to know Polish?

"Christopher," Mom said.

"What?" I asked.

"The card," Mom said.

"Dog," I said.

The tutor rubbed her eyebrows. She set the card underneath the stack. Mom excused me.

§§

Dad tries the next-door buzzer. A woman with blonde hair opens the door. Dad introduces us to her in Polish. But he doesn't need to. The woman, our old neighbor, puts her hand over her mouth like she can't believe it's us, even though Dad once again looks the same as always with his mustache. The woman welcomes us inside.

I follow Dad. I'm still concerned with my memory. I want to test it, to see if anything else changed. I know that the neighbor kid was nicknamed *Jeżyk*/Hedgehog because he had spiky hair. I ask this woman, his mother, if that's so.

Dad translates my question to the woman. And before she answers I already know from her slight smile pulling at her cheeks that it's true. She says, "*Tak, to jego przydomek*/Yes, that's his nickname."

I smile back. I'm glad that not everything is different. I look around the hallway as the woman and Dad catch up.

Honey-filled jars cover a side table. Their colors range from creamy-white to translucent-sunshine and to opaque-mustard. I remember the bees. The man of the house kept beehives. I wonder if the kids from the special needs school behind our house, whose park abutted our backyard fence, really set fire to our neighbor's hives. Did the melting hives ooze and Jeżyk's father try to put out the flames only with a garden hose?

I interrupt, asking if that fire happened. Dad translates. The woman nods, but without a smile. She looks away as she answers, like it's something too hard to remember.

A drizzle starts outside, returning Warsaw to the city I remember with heavy, close clouds. Dad and I buy a jar of raw honey before we leave. We run in the light rain, down the street, and away from our old house.

Dad and I make it to the overhang of a corner store just as the rain fully spills. Dad asks me what we should do. I say we should see if it lets up.

A few people with umbrellas walk by us on the wet sidewalk. Everything is gray. Above, the cement sky is the same as the city's foundations.

At home in Orlando, Mom has a watercolor of Old Town, showing the historic downtown market square in Warsaw. During World War II, when Nazi Germany occupied Poland, the Poles fought back in the Warsaw Uprising. After the resistance surrendered, Hitler commanded that the buildings of downtown Warsaw—the very framework of the capital—be destroyed.

After the war, the Poles rebuilt Old Town to make it look like it had before, as if the war had never happened. They based their replica off of paintings. The canvases must have looked like a dream of what once was.

I consider how a dozen years ago the fence at our house was huge to me, but then the fence became how it is. It seems the new replaced the old. But really, both memory and the moment can be true. I don't have to replace one with another.

The rain doesn't let up completely, but it lessens. I tell Dad we can go. I lead the way out of the neighborhood and back to the tram stop. The dirt path is damp and smells like wet clay, ready to be shaped.

§§

Chris Wiewiora spent his childhood in Warsaw, Poland with his parents who served as Evangelical missionaries behind the "Iron Curtain." Later, his parents moved their family to Orlando, Florida. Chris received Honors in the Major from the University of Central Florida where he worked as an assistant editor at *The Florida Review*. *The Distance Is More Than An Ocean* is his first chapbook. He wrote it while earning an MFA in Creative Writing and Environment at Iowa State University where he served as the managing editor of *Flyway: Journal of Writing and Environment*. After graduating, the National Endowment for Humanities deemed him a "Humanities Scholar" and Humanities Iowa awarded him a grant for hosting the radio show *BOOK CENTRAL* where he interviewed authors writing from the Central Time Zone. His nonfiction has been published in *Airplane Reading, A River & Sound Review, Essay Daily, Redivider, Slice,* and *Story* as well as anthologized in *Back to the Lake, Best American Sports Writing, Best Food Writing, The Norton Reader,* and *Two-Countries: U.S. Daughters and Sons of Immigrant Parents*. He regularly contributes to *The Good Men Project*. Read more at www.chriswiewiora.com

CPSIA information can be obtained
at www.ICGtesting.com
Printed in the USA
JSHW040831190520
5760JS00002B/161